THE REAL ESTATE AGENT'S 12-MONTH PLANNING WORKBOOK

THE MONTH-BY-MONTH PLANNER FOR MANAGING LEADS, CLIENTS, INCOME AND RESULTS

BRIDGET McCREA

STRONGTIDE PRESS

ISBN 978-0-578-54927-9 (paperback)

Published by StrongTide Press
www.strongtidepress.com
Printed and distributed in the United States of America

This book is for informational and educational purposes only. The author is not an attorney, accountant or financial advisor. The book is not meant to provide legal, tax or financial advice. Laws, rules and requirements change. Every business situation is different, so please consult a qualified professional for guidance specific to you.

Any products, services, URLs or organizations mentioned are included for reference only. The author has no affiliation, endorsement or agreements with them. Use your own judgment before acting on any information provided in the following pages.

STRONGTIDE
press

Ready to Start Your Strongest Year Yet?

I really wish I'd had this book when I got started in real estate. I was fresh out of college so the educational portion and licensing exam both went well. I passed on the first time out, hung my license with a well-known franchise and felt ready to launch a career in real estate.

I learned pretty quickly that passing an exam and actually earning a living in real estate were two completely different things. You need systems, support, a network of potential buyers and sellers, and hands-on knowledge to successfully break through that barrier. I had none of those things.

What I did have was an extremely nice managing broker who'd been in the business 20+ years and who sat down with me one night and showed me how to, 1) make sense of the thick MLS books that existed before online listings came along, and 2) contact the expired listings that came in on the dead sea scroll-esque fax machine every morning.

I was 20 years old, had no immediate circle of "friends and family" ready to list their properties or buy what I was selling. I also had zero sales experience. When a veteran agent walked into the office, took one look at me working floor duty and said (and I quote), "You're pretty young to be in this business, shouldn't you be in college instead?" my fragile ego shattered pretty quickly.

I went on to work in real estate for a while and later became an assistant to a successful Century 21 agent who showed me the ropes and gave me a firsthand education on all things real estate-related. My true calling wound up being freelance writing, but I didn't just forget about my years spent in real estate. In fact, I've contributed to REALTOR® Magazine and most of NAR's state real estate magazines (Texas, Florida, New Jersey, Illinois and others).

In 2005, the American Management Association (AMACOM) asked me to write the first edition of The Real Estate Agent's Business Planner. The 20th Anniversary Edition of that book published in 2025 now comes with free digital bonus planning tools and is the companion book to the one you're reading right now. So if you're in the market for a good business planning guide, be sure to check it out.

Along the way I've learned that real estate is a business that moves fast and expects you to keep up. Even with good training and strong guidance from brokers and mentors, it takes time to build a steady and predictable business. My goal with this workbook is to help shorten that learning curve and give you simple, practical tools that keep you focused on the work that moves your business forward.

This career is full of moving parts and it's easy to get pulled in different directions every day. Without a plan, you end up reacting instead of staying ahead of your work. These worksheets help you manage that complexity and see what's working, what's stalling and where your time and attention are best spent.

Use this workbook consistently to keep yourself organized, track your progress and stay connected to your goals. With each new month you'll build steady habits that strengthen your workflow from prospecting to follow up to managing your pipeline. This book won't do the work for you, but it will help you stay focused in a field where consistency and persistence both matter.

Stick with it and you'll set yourself up for your strongest year yet.

Get Focused. Get Organized. Get Moving.

This workbook includes five targeted forms for each month of the year. Each packet works as a complete operating system for your real estate business. Because you fill in the month and year, you can start whenever you want and set a pace that fits your workflow. Use the forms monthly if you want a close view of your activity or stretch them to a bimonthly or quarterly schedule if that works better for you.

The goal here is simple: Stay organized, focused and in control of your business.

→ **Form #1: New Client Prospecting Blueprint**

What This Form Helps You Do
Here's a clear way to track weekly outreach across calls, texts, emails, follow ups, real conversations and appointments. It includes space to record the 10 connections that matter most and a monthly pipeline check.

What You'll Get From This Form
Prospecting is powerful when you work it consistently. It can fall off your radar when everything else speeds up. This worksheet keeps you focused on simple actions that build conversations and create steady momentum. When you can see your weekly activity at a glance, you stay more confident and more aware of your progress.

How to Use This Form
- Record your totals for each week
- Track your 10 meaningful connections, not just busywork
- Review your pipeline and keep new leads flowing
- Use the self-assessment to strengthen your habits
- Note what worked so you can repeat it next month

→ **Form #2: Monthly Marketing Spend Tracker**

What This Form Helps You Do
Track your monthly marketing spend, the results it produced and where you may want to adjust.

What You'll Get From This Form
Every agent builds a marketing plan that fits their business. The strongest plans share one trait. They measure what each dollar produces. This tracker lays out your spending and the leads tied to each

category so you can see what works, what needs attention and what you may want to shift. You'll make clearer decisions and protect your budget with more confidence.

How to Use This Form

- Enter each category's spend and the leads it produced
- Total your spending and leads at the end of the month
- Calculate cost per lead and cost per closing
- Use "Keep or Cut" to guide your next steps
- Try one or two small adjustments and measure the results

→ Form #3: Financial Stability Check

What This Form Helps You Do

Get a grounded view of your financial picture each month and stay steady as your business grows.

What You'll Get From This Form

Real estate income rises and falls with your pipeline, and that pattern takes time to manage with confidence. This form helps you see what's coming in, what's going out and what needs attention right now. It helps you spot changes early so you can adjust before they impact your month and build healthy financial habits that support your long-term success.

How to Use This Form

- Start by recording your opening balance and expected income
- List all fixed expenses and note any changes
- Track discretionary spending so you can see patterns
- Update debt and savings to monitor your progress
- Use the red flag checklist to stay aware of stress points
- Choose one change that'll help you stay steady next month

→ Form #4: Lead Conversion Log

What This Form Helps You Do

Track each lead from the moment it arrives through follow ups, contact attempts, appointments and outcomes. Then do a follow-up check and a monthly review.

What You'll Get From This Form

Strong follow up builds trust and gets clients off the fence and into the market (with you as their trusted guide). This log keeps every detail in one place so you can respond quickly, track progress and stay organized. When you can see which leads need attention and which ones are moving, you gain more control over your workflow and your results.

How to Use This Form

- Log each lead as soon as it enters your system
- Track the first contact attempt and all follow ups
- Note when you make contact and when you set an appointment
- Mark each lead as converted or lost and record the reason
- Use the follow-up check to stay responsive
- Review what worked and what needs improvement

→ Form #5: Monthly Pipeline and Business Momentum Snapshot

What This Form Helps You Do

Keep an at-a-glance view of your clients, sources, stages, estimated income, next steps and wins for the month. It includes a monthly review, micro-goals, a market snapshot and three "get out of the office" activities.

What You'll Get From This Form

Agents who grow steadily tend to know exactly where their business stands. This dashboard helps you see your pipeline clearly, understand your income picture and stay on top of market shifts. When you have everything on one page, you can make better decisions, stay organized and keep your business on track.

How to Use This Form

- Update each client's stage and note the next step
- Review estimated income and note income at risk
- Complete the month-in-review to see what supported your progress
- Set three realistic micro-goals for yourself
- Fill in the market snapshot to stay current
- Choose three out-of-office activities that keep you visible in the community
- Use what you learned to guide next month's priorities

Month _____ Year_____

Form #1: Prospecting Worksheet

Your Hit List: Targets You Reached This Month

Activity	Week One	Week Two	Week Three	Week Four	Week Five	Total
Calls made						
Texts sent						
Emails sent						
Follow-ups completed						
Real conversations						
Appointments booked						

The 10 Connections that Mattered Most

         *Lead Type   Names(s) or Source   Notes

1) _____ _____ _____
2) _____ _____ _____
3) _____ _____ _____
4) _____ _____ _____
5) _____ _____ _____
6) _____ _____ _____
7) _____ _____ _____
8) _____ _____ _____
9) _____ _____ _____
10) _____ _____ _____

*Sphere of influence, online lead, open house, referral, past client, cold outreach, etc.

Your Pipeline Check

New leads added to CRM: _____

Warm leads contacted this month: _____

Cold leads reactivated: _____

Follow-up tasks scheduled for next month: _____

Quick Self-Assessment
(Circle one)

I stayed consistent:	YES	NO	SOMETIMES
I focused more on conversations than counting tasks:	YES	NO	SOMETIMES
I followed up when I said I would:	YES	NO	SOMETIMES
I protected my prospecting time:	YES	NO	SOMETIMES

What Moved the Needle this Month?

Which efforts generated the best conversations this month?

_____

_____

_____

_____

_____

Where did I lose focus or momentum and how can I gain it back?

_____

_____

_____

_____

_____

One adjustment I'll make next month:

_____

_____

_____

_____

_____

Form #2: Monthly Marketing Spend Tracker

Where Your Marketing Dollars are Going

Category	Amount Spent	Leads Generated	Notes
Ads - Facebook/Instagram	_____	_____	_____ _____
Ads - Google/YouTube	_____	_____	_____ _____
Print/Postcards	_____	_____	_____ _____
MLS/Tech Subscriptions	_____	_____	_____ _____
Lead Gen Platforms	_____	_____	_____ _____
Website/SEO	_____	_____	_____ _____
Email Marketing	_____	_____	_____ _____
Open House	_____	_____	_____ _____
Supplies	_____	_____	_____ _____
Client Gifts/Events	_____	_____	_____ _____
Misc.	_____	_____	_____ _____
TOTALS	_____	_____	_____ _____

Summary + Quick Calculations

Total Monthly Spend: $_____

Total Leads Generated: _____

Cost per Lead (CPL):
Total Spend ÷ Total Leads = $_____

Cost per Closing (CPC):
Total Spend ÷ # of Closings from This Month's Leads = $_____

Keep or Cut?

Which expenses earned their keep this month?

_____
_____
_____
_____
_____

Which expenses didn't deliver and should be dropped next month?

_____
_____
_____
_____
_____

What change will I make to improve ROI next month?

_____
_____
_____
_____
_____

Form #3: Financial Stability Check

Monthly Financial Snapshot

Opening Balance $ _____

Expected Income $ _____

Actual Income $ _____

Notes   _____

     _____

Fixed Expenses

	Amount
Rent/Mortgage	$ _____
Car Payment	$ _____
Insurance	$ _____
MLS/Association Dues	$ _____
Phone/Internet	$ _____
CRM/Software	$ _____
Advertising Subscriptions	$ _____
Utilities	$ _____
Other	$ _____

Discretionary Spending

Item	Amount
_____	$ _____
_____	$ _____
_____	$ _____
_____	$ _____
_____	$ _____
_____	$ _____

Debt/Savings Update

Debt Changes (increase or decrease) _____

Current Savings Balance $ _____

Savings Added This Month $ _____

Red Flag Check

[ ] I spent more than I earned

[ ] I didn't track my expenses

[ ] I relied on credit to get through the month

[ ] My savings dropped instead of increasing

[ ] I struggled to cover fixed expenses

What's Working & What's Not

Where did I stay financially disciplined this month?

_____
_____
_____
_____
_____

Where did I lose focus or overspend?

_____
_____
_____
_____
_____

One adjustment I'll make next month:

_____
_____
_____
_____
_____

Form #4: Lead Conversion Log

Lead Name	Source	Date Recieved	First Contact Attempt	Follow-up Attempts	Appointment Set (Y/N)	Converted or Lost

Lead Details Snapshot

Lead Name	Source	Status

Your Follow-Up Check

New leads added this month: _____

Leads contacted within 24 hours: _____

Leads requiring additional follow-up: _____

Appointments scheduled: _____

Closed deals from this month's leads: _____

Quick Self-Assessment

I responded to leads quickly:	YES	NO	SOMETIMES
I stayed consistent with my follow-up:	YES	NO	SOMETIMES
I used the right number of touchpoints:	YES	NO	SOMETIMES
I handled objections clearly and confidently:	YES	NO	SOMETIMES
I protected my lead follow-up time:	YES	NO	SOMETIMES

What's Working & What's Not

What generated the best conversations this month?

_____

_____

_____

_____

_____

Where did my follow-up slow down or fall through?

_____

_____

_____

_____

_____

One small-but-mighty adjustment I will make next month:

_____

_____

_____

_____

_____

Form #5: Monthly Pipeline & Momentum Dashboard

Pipeline + Money Flow

Client	Source	Stage (New, Warm, Hot, Pending)	Actions Needed	Est. Close	Est. $	Confidence Level

Projected Income: _____

Income at Risk (i.e., deals that may not close on time): _____

Closed Deals This Month: _____

This Month in Review

What worked?

_____
_____
_____
_____

What didn't?

_____
_____
_____
_____

Keep:

_____
_____
_____
_____

Drop:

_____
_____
_____
_____

Three Micro-Goals for This Month:

1) _____

2) _____

3) _____

Market & Competitor Snapshot

New listings: _____

Closings: _____

Days on market: _____

Trend: _____

Competitor move worth noting: _____

Three "Get Out of the Office" Activities

Examples:
- Visit a local business owner to check in.
- Preview two new listings for market awareness.
- Walk your farm area and talk to three homeowners.
- Drop off a CMA packet to a warm lead.
- Attend one community or networking event.

1. _____

2. _____

3. _____

Month _____ Year_____

Form #1: Prospecting Worksheet

Your Hit List: Targets You Reached This Month

Activity	Week One	Week Two	Week Three	Week Four	Week Five	Total
Calls made						
Texts sent						
Emails sent						
Follow-ups completed						
Real conversations						
Appointments booked						

The 10 Connections that Mattered Most

	*Lead Type	Names(s) or Source	Notes
1)			
2)			
3)			
4)			
5)			
6)			
7)			
8)			
9)			
10)			

*Sphere of influence, online lead, open house, referral, past client, cold outreach, etc.

Your Pipeline Check

New leads added to CRM: _____

Warm leads contacted this month: _____

Cold leads reactivated: _____

Follow-up tasks scheduled for next month: _____

Quick Self-Assessment
(Circle one)

I stayed consistent:	YES	NO	SOMETIMES
I focused more on conversations than counting tasks:	YES	NO	SOMETIMES
I followed up when I said I would:	YES	NO	SOMETIMES
I protected my prospecting time:	YES	NO	SOMETIMES

What Moved the Needle this Month?

Which efforts generated the best conversations this month?

_____
_____
_____
_____
_____

Where did I lose focus or momentum and how can I gain it back?

_____
_____
_____
_____
_____

One adjustment I'll make next month:

_____
_____
_____
_____
_____

Form #2: Monthly Marketing Spend Tracker

Where Your Marketing Dollars are Going

Category	Amount Spent	Leads Generated	Notes
Ads - Facebook/Instagram	_____	_____	_____ _____
Ads - Google/YouTube	_____	_____	_____ _____
Print/Postcards	_____	_____	_____ _____
MLS/Tech Subscriptions	_____	_____	_____ _____
Lead Gen Platforms	_____	_____	_____ _____
Website/SEO	_____	_____	_____ _____
Email Marketing	_____	_____	_____ _____
Open House	_____	_____	_____ _____
Supplies	_____	_____	_____ _____
Client Gifts/Events	_____	_____	_____ _____
Misc.	_____	_____	_____ _____
TOTALS	_____	_____	_____ _____

Summary + Quick Calculations

Total Monthly Spend: $_____

Total Leads Generated: _____

Cost per Lead (CPL):
Total Spend ÷ Total Leads = $_____

Cost per Closing (CPC):
Total Spend ÷ # of Closings from This Month's Leads = $_____

Keep or Cut?

Which expenses earned their keep this month?

_____
_____
_____
_____
_____

Which expenses didn't deliver and should be dropped next month?

_____
_____
_____
_____
_____

What change will I make to improve ROI next month?

_____
_____
_____
_____
_____

Form #3: Financial Stability Check

Monthly Financial Snapshot

Opening Balance $ _____

Expected Income $ _____

Actual Income $ _____

Notes   _____

_____

Fixed Expenses

Amount

Rent/Mortgage $ _____

Car Payment $ _____

Insurance $ _____

MLS/Association Dues $ _____

Phone/Internet $ _____

CRM/Software $ _____

Advertising Subscriptions $ _____

Utilities $ _____

Other $ _____

Discretionary Spending

Item   **Amount**

_____ $ _____

_____ $ _____

_____ $ _____

_____ $ _____

_____ $ _____

_____ $ _____

Debt/Savings Update

Debt Changes (increase or decrease) _____

Current Savings Balance $ _____

Savings Added This Month $ _____

Red Flag Check

[ ] I spent more than I earned

[ ] I didn't track my expenses

[ ] I relied on credit to get through the month

[ ] My savings dropped instead of increasing

[ ] I struggled to cover fixed expenses

What's Working & What's Not

Where did I stay financially disciplined this month?

_____
_____
_____
_____
_____

Where did I lose focus or overspend?

_____
_____
_____
_____
_____

One adjustment I'll make next month:

_____
_____
_____
_____
_____

Form #4: Lead Conversion Log

Lead Name	Source	Date Recieved	First Contact Attempt	Follow-up Attempts	Appointment Set (Y/N)	Converted or Lost

Lead Details Snapshot

Lead Name	Source	Status

Your Follow-Up Check

New leads added this month: _____

Leads contacted within 24 hours: _____

Leads requiring additional follow-up: _____

Appointments scheduled: _____

Closed deals from this month's leads: _____

Quick Self-Assessment

I responded to leads quickly:	YES	NO	SOMETIMES
I stayed consistent with my follow-up:	YES	NO	SOMETIMES
I used the right number of touchpoints:	YES	NO	SOMETIMES
I handled objections clearly and confidently:	YES	NO	SOMETIMES
I protected my lead follow-up time:	YES	NO	SOMETIMES

What's Working & What's Not

What generated the best conversations this month?

_____

_____

_____

_____

_____

Where did my follow-up slow down or fall through?

_____

_____

_____

_____

_____

One small-but-mighty adjustment I will make next month:

_____

_____

_____

_____

_____

Form #5: Monthly Pipeline & Momentum Dashboard

Pipeline + Money Flow

Client	Source	Stage (New, Warm, Hot, Pending)	Actions Needed	Est. Close	Est. $	Confidence Level

Projected Income: _____

Income at Risk (i.e., deals that may not close on time): _____

Closed Deals This Month: _____

This Month in Review

What worked?

_____
_____
_____
_____

What didn't?

_____
_____
_____
_____

Keep:

_____
_____
_____
_____

Drop:

_____
_____
_____
_____

Three Micro-Goals for This Month:

1) _____

2) _____

3) _____

Market & Competitor Snapshot

New listings: _____

Closings: _____

Days on market: _____

Trend: _____

Competitor move worth noting: _____

Three "Get Out of the Office" Activities

Examples:
- Visit a local business owner to check in.
- Preview two new listings for market awareness.
- Walk your farm area and talk to three homeowners.
- Drop off a CMA packet to a warm lead.
- Attend one community or networking event.

1. _____

2. _____

3. _____

Month _____ Year _____

Form #1: Prospecting Worksheet

Your Hit List: Targets You Reached This Month

Activity	Week One	Week Two	Week Three	Week Four	Week Five	Total
Calls made						
Texts sent						
Emails sent						
Follow-ups completed						
Real conversations						
Appointments booked						

The 10 Connections that Mattered Most

	*Lead Type	Names(s) or Source	Notes
1)	_____	_____	_____
2)	_____	_____	_____
3)	_____	_____	_____
4)	_____	_____	_____
5)	_____	_____	_____
6)	_____	_____	_____
7)	_____	_____	_____
8)	_____	_____	_____
9)	_____	_____	_____
10)	_____	_____	_____

*Sphere of influence, online lead, open house, referral, past client, cold outreach, etc.

Your Pipeline Check

New leads added to CRM: _____

Warm leads contacted this month: _____

Cold leads reactivated: _____

Follow-up tasks scheduled for next month: _____

Quick Self-Assessment
(Circle one)

I stayed consistent:	YES	NO	SOMETIMES
I focused more on conversations than counting tasks:	YES	NO	SOMETIMES
I followed up when I said I would:	YES	NO	SOMETIMES
I protected my prospecting time:	YES	NO	SOMETIMES

What Moved the Needle this Month?

Which efforts generated the best conversations this month?

_____
_____
_____
_____
_____

Where did I lose focus or momentum and how can I gain it back?

_____
_____
_____
_____
_____

One adjustment I'll make next month:

_____
_____
_____
_____
_____

Form #2: Monthly Marketing Spend Tracker

Where Your Marketing Dollars are Going

Category	Amount Spent	Leads Generated	Notes
Ads – Facebook/Instagram	_____	_____	_____ _____
Ads – Google/YouTube	_____	_____	_____ _____
Print/Postcards	_____	_____	_____ _____
MLS/Tech Subscriptions	_____	_____	_____ _____
Lead Gen Platforms	_____	_____	_____ _____
Website/SEO	_____	_____	_____ _____
Email Marketing	_____	_____	_____ _____
Open House	_____	_____	_____ _____
Supplies	_____	_____	_____ _____
Client Gifts/Events	_____	_____	_____ _____
Misc.	_____	_____	_____ _____
TOTALS	_____	_____	_____ _____

Summary + Quick Calculations

Total Monthly Spend: $_____

Total Leads Generated: _____

Cost per Lead (CPL):
Total Spend ÷ Total Leads = $_____

Cost per Closing (CPC):
Total Spend ÷ # of Closings from This Month's Leads = $_____

Keep or Cut? ✂

Which expenses earned their keep this month?

_____
_____
_____
_____
_____

Which expenses didn't deliver and should be dropped next month?

_____
_____
_____
_____
_____

What change will I make to improve ROI next month?

_____
_____
_____
_____
_____

Form #3: Financial Stability Check

Monthly Financial Snapshot

Opening Balance $ _____

Expected Income $ _____

Actual Income $ _____

Notes   _____

_____

Fixed Expenses

	Amount
Rent/Mortgage	$ _____
Car Payment	$ _____
Insurance	$ _____
MLS/Association Dues	$ _____
Phone/Internet	$ _____
CRM/Software	$ _____
Advertising Subscriptions	$ _____
Utilities	$ _____
Other	$ _____

Discretionary Spending

Item	Amount
_____	$ _____
_____	$ _____
_____	$ _____
_____	$ _____
_____	$ _____
_____	$ _____

Debt/Savings Update

Debt Changes (increase or decrease)   _____

Current Savings Balance $ _____

Savings Added This Month $ _____

Red Flag Check

[ ] I spent more than I earned

[ ] I didn't track my expenses

[ ] I relied on credit to get through the month

[ ] My savings dropped instead of increasing

[ ] I struggled to cover fixed expenses

What's Working & What's Not

Where did I stay financially disciplined this month?

_____
_____
_____
_____
_____

Where did I lose focus or overspend?

_____
_____
_____
_____
_____

One adjustment I'll make next month:

_____
_____
_____
_____
_____

Form #4: Lead Conversion Log

Lead Name	Source	Date Recieved	First Contact Attempt	Follow-up Attempts	Appointment Set (Y/N)	Converted or Lost

Lead Details Snapshot

Lead Name	Source	Status

Your Follow-Up Check

New leads added this month: _____

Leads contacted within 24 hours: _____

Leads requiring additional follow-up: _____

Appointments scheduled: _____

Closed deals from this month's leads: _____

Quick Self-Assessment

I responded to leads quickly:	YES	NO	SOMETIMES
I stayed consistent with my follow-up:	YES	NO	SOMETIMES
I used the right number of touchpoints:	YES	NO	SOMETIMES
I handled objections clearly and confidently:	YES	NO	SOMETIMES
I protected my lead follow-up time:	YES	NO	SOMETIMES

What's Working & What's Not

What generated the best conversations this month?

_____
_____
_____
_____
_____

Where did my follow-up slow down or fall through?

_____
_____
_____
_____
_____

One small-but-mighty adjustment I will make next month:

_____
_____
_____
_____
_____

Form #5: Monthly Pipeline & Momentum Dashboard

Pipeline + Money Flow

Client	Source	Stage (New, Warm, Hot, Pending)	Actions Needed	Est. Close	Est. $	Confidence Level

Projected Income: _____

Income at Risk (i.e., deals that may not close on time): _____

Closed Deals This Month: _____

This Month in Review

What worked?

_____

_____

_____

_____

What didn't?

_____

_____

_____

_____

Keep:

_____

_____

_____

_____

Drop:

_____

_____

_____

_____

Three Micro-Goals for This Month:

1) _____

2) _____

3) _____

Market & Competitor Snapshot

New listings: _____

Closings: _____

Days on market: _____

Trend: _____

Competitor move worth noting: _____

Three "Get Out of the Office" Activities

Examples:
- Visit a local business owner to check in.
- Preview two new listings for market awareness.
- Walk your farm area and talk to three homeowners.
- Drop off a CMA packet to a warm lead.
- Attend one community or networking event.

1. _____

2. _____

3. _____

Month _____ Year_____

Form #1: Prospecting Worksheet

Your Hit List: Targets You Reached This Month

Activity	Week One	Week Two	Week Three	Week Four	Week Five	Total
Calls made						
Texts sent						
Emails sent						
Follow-ups completed						
Real conversations						
Appointments booked						

The 10 Connections that Mattered Most

	*Lead Type	Names(s) or Source	Notes
1)	_____	_____	_____
2)	_____	_____	_____
3)	_____	_____	_____
4)	_____	_____	_____
5)	_____	_____	_____
6)	_____	_____	_____
7)	_____	_____	_____
8)	_____	_____	_____
9)	_____	_____	_____
10)	_____	_____	_____

*Sphere of influence, online lead, open house, referral, past client, cold outreach, etc.

Your Pipeline Check

New leads added to CRM: _____

Warm leads contacted this month: _____

Cold leads reactivated: _____

Follow-up tasks scheduled for next month: _____

Quick Self-Assessment
(Circle one)

I stayed consistent:	YES	NO	SOMETIMES
I focused more on conversations than counting tasks:	YES	NO	SOMETIMES
I followed up when I said I would:	YES	NO	SOMETIMES
I protected my prospecting time:	YES	NO	SOMETIMES

What Moved the Needle this Month?

Which efforts generated the best conversations this month?

_____
_____
_____
_____
_____

Where did I lose focus or momentum and how can I gain it back?

_____
_____
_____
_____
_____

One adjustment I'll make next month:

_____
_____
_____
_____
_____

Form #2: Monthly Marketing Spend Tracker

Where Your Marketing Dollars are Going

Category	Amount Spent	Leads Generated	Notes
Ads – Facebook/Instagram			
Ads – Google/YouTube			
Print/Postcards			
MLS/Tech Subscriptions			
Lead Gen Platforms			
Website/SEO			
Email Marketing			
Open House			
Supplies			
Client Gifts/Events			
Misc.			
TOTALS			

Summary + Quick Calculations

Total Monthly Spend: $_____

Total Leads Generated: _____

Cost per Lead (CPL):
Total Spend ÷ Total Leads = $_____

Cost per Closing (CPC):
Total Spend ÷ # of Closings from This Month's Leads = $_____

Keep or Cut? ✂

Which expenses earned their keep this month?

_____
_____
_____
_____
_____

Which expenses didn't deliver and should be dropped next month?

_____
_____
_____
_____
_____

What change will I make to improve ROI next month?

_____
_____
_____
_____
_____

Form #3: Financial Stability Check

Monthly Financial Snapshot

Opening Balance $ _____

Expected Income $ _____

Actual Income $ _____

Notes _____

_____

Fixed Expenses

	Amount
Rent/Mortgage	$ _____
Car Payment	$ _____
Insurance	$ _____
MLS/Association Dues	$ _____
Phone/Internet	$ _____
CRM/Software	$ _____
Advertising Subscriptions	$ _____
Utilities	$ _____
Other	$ _____

Discretionary Spending

Item	Amount
_____	$ _____
_____	$ _____
_____	$ _____
_____	$ _____
_____	$ _____
_____	$ _____

Debt/Savings Update

Debt Changes (increase or decrease) _____

Current Savings Balance $ _____

Savings Added This Month $ _____

Red Flag Check

[ ] I spent more than I earned

[ ] I didn't track my expenses

[ ] I relied on credit to get through the month

[ ] My savings dropped instead of increasing

[ ] I struggled to cover fixed expenses

What's Working & What's Not

Where did I stay financially disciplined this month?

_____
_____
_____
_____
_____

Where did I lose focus or overspend?

_____
_____
_____
_____
_____

One adjustment I'll make next month:

_____
_____
_____
_____

Form #4: Lead Conversion Log

Lead Name	Source	Date Recieved	First Contact Attempt	Follow-up Attempts	Appointment Set (Y/N)	Converted or Lost

Lead Details Snapshot

Lead Name	Source	Status

Your Follow-Up Check

New leads added this month: _____

Leads contacted within 24 hours: _____

Leads requiring additional follow-up: _____

Appointments scheduled: _____

Closed deals from this month's leads: _____

Quick Self-Assessment

I responded to leads quickly: YES   NO   SOMETIMES

I stayed consistent with my follow-up: YES   NO   SOMETIMES

I used the right number of touchpoints: YES   NO   SOMETIMES

I handled objections clearly and confidently: YES   NO   SOMETIMES

I protected my lead follow-up time: YES   NO   SOMETIMES

What's Working & What's Not

What generated the best conversations this month?

_____

_____

_____

_____

_____

Where did my follow-up slow down or fall through?

_____

_____

_____

_____

_____

One small-but-mighty adjustment I will make next month:

_____

_____

_____

_____

_____

Form #5: Monthly Pipeline & Momentum Dashboard

Pipeline + Money Flow

Client	Source	Stage (New, Warm, Hot, Pending)	Actions Needed	Est. Close	Est. $	Confidence Level

Projected Income: _____

Income at Risk (i.e., deals that may not close on time): _____

Closed Deals This Month: _____

This Month in Review

What worked?

_____

_____

_____

_____

What didn't?

_____

_____

_____

_____

Keep:

_____
_____
_____
_____

Drop:

_____
_____
_____
_____

Three Micro-Goals for This Month:

1) _____

2) _____

3) _____

Market & Competitor Snapshot

New listings: _____

Closings: _____

Days on market: _____

Trend: _____

Competitor move worth noting: _____

Three "Get Out of the Office" Activities

Examples:
- Visit a local business owner to check in.
- Preview two new listings for market awareness.
- Walk your farm area and talk to three homeowners.
- Drop off a CMA packet to a warm lead.
- Attend one community or networking event.

1. _____

2. _____

3. _____

Month _____ Year_____

Form #1: Prospecting Worksheet

Your Hit List: Targets You Reached This Month

Activity	Week One	Week Two	Week Three	Week Four	Week Five	Total
Calls made						
Texts sent						
Emails sent						
Follow-ups completed						
Real conversations						
Appointments booked						

The 10 Connections that Mattered Most

	*Lead Type	Names(s) or Source	Notes
1)	_____	_____	_____
2)	_____	_____	_____
3)	_____	_____	_____
4)	_____	_____	_____
5)	_____	_____	_____
6)	_____	_____	_____
7)	_____	_____	_____
8)	_____	_____	_____
9)	_____	_____	_____
10)	_____	_____	_____

*Sphere of influence, online lead, open house, referral, past client, cold outreach, etc.

Your Pipeline Check

New leads added to CRM: _____

Warm leads contacted this month: _____

Cold leads reactivated: _____

Follow-up tasks scheduled for next month: _____

Quick Self-Assessment
(Circle one)

I stayed consistent:	YES	NO	SOMETIMES
I focused more on conversations than counting tasks:	YES	NO	SOMETIMES
I followed up when I said I would:	YES	NO	SOMETIMES
I protected my prospecting time:	YES	NO	SOMETIMES

What Moved the Needle this Month?

Which efforts generated the best conversations this month?

_____
_____
_____
_____
_____

Where did I lose focus or momentum and how can I gain it back?

_____
_____
_____
_____
_____

One adjustment I'll make next month:

_____
_____
_____
_____
_____

Form #2: Monthly Marketing Spend Tracker

Where Your Marketing Dollars are Going

Category	Amount Spent	Leads Generated	Notes
Ads – Facebook/Instagram			
Ads – Google/YouTube			
Print/Postcards			
MLS/Tech Subscriptions			
Lead Gen Platforms			
Website/SEO			
Email Marketing			
Open House			
Supplies			
Client Gifts/Events			
Misc.			
TOTALS			

Summary + Quick Calculations

Total Monthly Spend: $_____

Total Leads Generated: _____

Cost per Lead (CPL):
Total Spend ÷ Total Leads = $_____

Cost per Closing (CPC):
Total Spend ÷ # of Closings from This Month's Leads = $_____

Keep or Cut?

Which expenses earned their keep this month?

_____
_____
_____
_____
_____

Which expenses didn't deliver and should be dropped next month?

_____
_____
_____
_____
_____

What change will I make to improve ROI next month?

_____
_____
_____
_____
_____

Form #3: Financial Stability Check

Monthly Financial Snapshot

Opening Balance $ _____

Expected Income $ _____

Actual Income $ _____

Notes   _____

_____

Fixed Expenses

Amount

Rent/Mortgage $ _____

Car Payment $ _____

Insurance $ _____

MLS/Association Dues $ _____

Phone/Internet $ _____

CRM/Software $ _____

Advertising Subscriptions $ _____

Utilities $ _____

Other $ _____

Discretionary Spending

Item   **Amount**

_____ $ _____

_____ $ _____

_____ $ _____

_____ $ _____

_____ $ _____

_____ $ _____

Debt/Savings Update

Debt Changes (increase or decrease) _____

Current Savings Balance $ _____

Savings Added This Month $ _____

Red Flag Check

[ ] I spent more than I earned

[ ] I didn't track my expenses

[ ] I relied on credit to get through the month

[ ] My savings dropped instead of increasing

[ ] I struggled to cover fixed expenses

What's Working & What's Not

Where did I stay financially disciplined this month?

_____
_____
_____
_____
_____

Where did I lose focus or overspend?

_____
_____
_____
_____
_____

One adjustment I'll make next month:

_____
_____
_____
_____
_____

Form #4: Lead Conversion Log

Lead Name	Source	Date Recieved	First Contact Attempt	Follow-up Attempts	Appointment Set (Y/N)	Converted or Lost

Lead Details Snapshot

Lead Name	Source	Status

Your Follow-Up Check

New leads added this month: _____

Leads contacted within 24 hours: _____

Leads requiring additional follow-up: _____

Appointments scheduled: _____

Closed deals from this month's leads: _____

Quick Self-Assessment

I responded to leads quickly:	YES	NO	SOMETIMES
I stayed consistent with my follow-up:	YES	NO	SOMETIMES
I used the right number of touchpoints:	YES	NO	SOMETIMES
I handled objections clearly and confidently:	YES	NO	SOMETIMES
I protected my lead follow-up time:	YES	NO	SOMETIMES

What's Working & What's Not

What generated the best conversations this month?

_____
_____
_____
_____
_____

Where did my follow-up slow down or fall through?

_____
_____
_____
_____
_____

One small-but-mighty adjustment I will make next month:

_____
_____
_____
_____
_____

Form #5: Monthly Pipeline & Momentum Dashboard

Pipeline + Money Flow

Client	Source	Stage (New, Warm, Hot, Pending)	Actions Needed	Est. Close	Est. $	Confidence Level

Projected Income: _____

Income at Risk (i.e., deals that may not close on time): _____

Closed Deals This Month: _____

This Month in Review

What worked?

_____

_____

_____

_____

What didn't?

_____

_____

_____

_____

Keep:

_____
_____
_____
_____

Drop:

_____
_____
_____
_____

Three Micro-Goals for This Month:

1) _____

2) _____

3) _____

Market & Competitor Snapshot

New listings: _____

Closings: _____

Days on market: _____

Trend: _____

Competitor move worth noting: _____

Three "Get Out of the Office" Activities

Examples:
- Visit a local business owner to check in.
- Preview two new listings for market awareness.
- Walk your farm area and talk to three homeowners.
- Drop off a CMA packet to a warm lead.
- Attend one community or networking event.

1. _____

2. _____

3. _____

Month _____ Year_____

Form #1: Prospecting Worksheet

Your Hit List: Targets You Reached This Month

Activity	Week One	Week Two	Week Three	Week Four	Week Five	Total
Calls made						
Texts sent						
Emails sent						
Follow-ups completed						
Real conversations						
Appointments booked						

The 10 Connections that Mattered Most

	*Lead Type	Names(s) or Source	Notes
1)			
2)			
3)			
4)			
5)			
6)			
7)			
8)			
9)			
10)			

*Sphere of influence, online lead, open house, referral, past client, cold outreach, etc.

Your Pipeline Check

New leads added to CRM: _____

Warm leads contacted this month: _____

Cold leads reactivated: _____

Follow-up tasks scheduled for next month: _____

Quick Self-Assessment
(Circle one)

I stayed consistent:	YES	NO	SOMETIMES
I focused more on conversations than counting tasks:	YES	NO	SOMETIMES
I followed up when I said I would:	YES	NO	SOMETIMES
I protected my prospecting time:	YES	NO	SOMETIMES

What Moved the Needle this Month?

Which efforts generated the best conversations this month?

_____
_____
_____
_____
_____

Where did I lose focus or momentum and how can I gain it back?

_____
_____
_____
_____
_____

One adjustment I'll make next month:

_____
_____
_____
_____
_____

Form #2: Monthly Marketing Spend Tracker

Where Your Marketing Dollars are Going

Category	Amount Spent	Leads Generated	Notes
Ads - Facebook/Instagram	_____	_____	_____
			_____
Ads - Google/YouTube	_____	_____	_____
			_____
Print/Postcards	_____	_____	_____
			_____
MLS/Tech Subscriptions	_____	_____	_____
			_____
Lead Gen Platforms	_____	_____	_____
			_____
Website/SEO	_____	_____	_____
			_____
Email Marketing	_____	_____	_____
			_____
Open House	_____	_____	_____
			_____
Supplies	_____	_____	_____
			_____
Client Gifts/Events	_____	_____	_____
			_____
Misc.	_____	_____	_____
			_____
TOTALS	_____	_____	_____
			_____

Summary + Quick Calculations

Total Monthly Spend: $_____

Total Leads Generated: _____

Cost per Lead (CPL):
Total Spend ÷ Total Leads = $_____

Cost per Closing (CPC):
Total Spend ÷ # of Closings from This Month's Leads = $_____

Keep or Cut?

Which expenses earned their keep this month?

_____
_____
_____
_____
_____

Which expenses didn't deliver and should be dropped next month?

_____
_____
_____
_____
_____

What change will I make to improve ROI next month?

_____
_____
_____
_____
_____

Form #3: Financial Stability Check

Monthly Financial Snapshot

Opening Balance $ _____

Expected Income $ _____

Actual Income $ _____

Notes   _____

_____

Fixed Expenses

Amount

Rent/Mortgage $ _____

Car Payment $ _____

Insurance $ _____

MLS/Association Dues $ _____

Phone/Internet $ _____

CRM/Software $ _____

Advertising Subscriptions $ _____

Utilities $ _____

Other $ _____

Discretionary Spending

Item   **Amount**

_____ $ _____

_____ $ _____

_____ $ _____

_____ $ _____

_____ $ _____

_____ $ _____

Debt/Savings Update

Debt Changes (increase or decrease) _____

Current Savings Balance $ _____

Savings Added This Month $ _____

Red Flag Check

[ ] I spent more than I earned

[ ] I didn't track my expenses

[ ] I relied on credit to get through the month

[ ] My savings dropped instead of increasing

[ ] I struggled to cover fixed expenses

What's Working & What's Not

Where did I stay financially disciplined this month?

_____
_____
_____
_____
_____

Where did I lose focus or overspend?

_____
_____
_____
_____
_____

One adjustment I'll make next month:

_____
_____
_____
_____
_____

Form #4: Lead Conversion Log

Lead Name	Source	Date Recieved	First Contact Attempt	Follow-up Attempts	Appointment Set (Y/N)	Converted or Lost

Lead Details Snapshot

Lead Name	Source	Status

Your Follow-Up Check

New leads added this month: _____

Leads contacted within 24 hours: _____

Leads requiring additional follow-up: _____

Appointments scheduled: _____

Closed deals from this month's leads: _____

Quick Self-Assessment

I responded to leads quickly:	YES	NO	SOMETIMES
I stayed consistent with my follow-up:	YES	NO	SOMETIMES
I used the right number of touchpoints:	YES	NO	SOMETIMES
I handled objections clearly and confidently:	YES	NO	SOMETIMES
I protected my lead follow-up time:	YES	NO	SOMETIMES

What's Working & What's Not

What generated the best conversations this month?

_____

_____

_____

_____

_____

Where did my follow-up slow down or fall through?

_____

_____

_____

_____

_____

One small-but-mighty adjustment I will make next month:

_____

_____

_____

_____

_____

Form #5: Monthly Pipeline & Momentum Dashboard

Pipeline + Money Flow

Client	Source	Stage (New, Warm, Hot, Pending)	Actions Needed	Est. Close	Est. $	Confidence Level

Projected Income: _____

Income at Risk (i.e., deals that may not close on time): _____

Closed Deals This Month: _____

This Month in Review

What worked?

_____

_____

_____

_____

What didn't?

_____

_____

_____

_____

Keep:

_____
_____
_____
_____

Drop:

_____
_____
_____
_____

Three Micro-Goals for This Month:

1) _____

2) _____

3) _____

Market & Competitor Snapshot

New listings: _____

Closings: _____

Days on market: _____

Trend: _____

Competitor move worth noting: _____

Three "Get Out of the Office" Activities

Examples:
- Visit a local business owner to check in.
- Preview two new listings for market awareness.
- Walk your farm area and talk to three homeowners.
- Drop off a CMA packet to a warm lead.
- Attend one community or networking event.

1. _____

2. _____

3. _____

Month _____ Year_____

Form #1: Prospecting Worksheet

Your Hit List: Targets You Reached This Month

Activity	Week One	Week Two	Week Three	Week Four	Week Five	Total
Calls made						
Texts sent						
Emails sent						
Follow-ups completed						
Real conversations						
Appointments booked						

The 10 Connections that Mattered Most

	*Lead Type	Names(s) or Source	Notes
1)			
2)			
3)			
4)			
5)			
6)			
7)			
8)			
9)			
10)			

*Sphere of influence, online lead, open house, referral, past client, cold outreach, etc.

Your Pipeline Check

New leads added to CRM: _____

Warm leads contacted this month: _____

Cold leads reactivated: _____

Follow-up tasks scheduled for next month: _____

Quick Self-Assessment
(Circle one)

I stayed consistent:	YES	NO	SOMETIMES
I focused more on conversations than counting tasks:	YES	NO	SOMETIMES
I followed up when I said I would:	YES	NO	SOMETIMES
I protected my prospecting time:	YES	NO	SOMETIMES

What Moved the Needle this Month?

Which efforts generated the best conversations this month?

_____
_____
_____
_____
_____

Where did I lose focus or momentum and how can I gain it back?

_____
_____
_____
_____
_____

One adjustment I'll make next month:

_____
_____
_____
_____
_____

Form #2: Monthly Marketing Spend Tracker

Where Your Marketing Dollars are Going

Category	Amount Spent	Leads Generated	Notes
Ads – Facebook/Instagram			
Ads – Google/YouTube			
Print/Postcards			
MLS/Tech Subscriptions			
Lead Gen Platforms			
Website/SEO			
Email Marketing			
Open House			
Supplies			
Client Gifts/Events			
Misc.			
TOTALS			

Summary + Quick Calculations

Total Monthly Spend: $_____

Total Leads Generated: _____

Cost per Lead (CPL):
Total Spend ÷ Total Leads = $_____

Cost per Closing (CPC):
Total Spend ÷ # of Closings from This Month's Leads = $_____

Keep or Cut? ✂

Which expenses earned their keep this month?

_____
_____
_____
_____
_____

Which expenses didn't deliver and should be dropped next month?

_____
_____
_____
_____
_____

What change will I make to improve ROI next month?

_____
_____
_____
_____
_____

Form #3: Financial Stability Check

Monthly Financial Snapshot

Opening Balance $ _____

Expected Income $ _____

Actual Income $ _____

Notes   _____

_____

Fixed Expenses

Amount

Rent/Mortgage $ _____

Car Payment $ _____

Insurance $ _____

MLS/Association Dues $ _____

Phone/Internet $ _____

CRM/Software $ _____

Advertising Subscriptions $ _____

Utilities $ _____

Other $ _____

Discretionary Spending

Item   **Amount**

_____ $ _____

_____ $ _____

_____ $ _____

_____ $ _____

_____ $ _____

_____ $ _____

Debt/Savings Update

Debt Changes (increase or decrease) _____

Current Savings Balance $ _____

Savings Added This Month $ _____

Red Flag Check

[ ] I spent more than I earned

[ ] I didn't track my expenses

[ ] I relied on credit to get through the month

[ ] My savings dropped instead of increasing

[ ] I struggled to cover fixed expenses

What's Working & What's Not

Where did I stay financially disciplined this month?

_____
_____
_____
_____
_____

Where did I lose focus or overspend?

_____
_____
_____
_____
_____

One adjustment I'll make next month:

_____
_____
_____
_____
_____

Form #4: Lead Conversion Log

Lead Name	Source	Date Recieved	First Contact Attempt	Follow-up Attempts	Appointment Set (Y/N)	Converted or Lost

Lead Details Snapshot

Lead Name	Source	Status

Your Follow-Up Check

New leads added this month: _____

Leads contacted within 24 hours: _____

Leads requiring additional follow-up: _____

Appointments scheduled: _____

Closed deals from this month's leads: _____

Quick Self-Assessment

I responded to leads quickly:	YES	NO	SOMETIMES
I stayed consistent with my follow-up:	YES	NO	SOMETIMES
I used the right number of touchpoints:	YES	NO	SOMETIMES
I handled objections clearly and confidently:	YES	NO	SOMETIMES
I protected my lead follow-up time:	YES	NO	SOMETIMES

What's Working & What's Not

What generated the best conversations this month?

_____

_____

_____

_____

_____

Where did my follow-up slow down or fall through?

_____

_____

_____

_____

_____

One small-but-mighty adjustment I will make next month:

_____

_____

_____

_____

_____

Form #5: Monthly Pipeline & Momentum Dashboard

Pipeline + Money Flow

Client	Source	Stage (New, Warm, Hot, Pending)	Actions Needed	Est. Close	Est. $	Confidence Level

Projected Income: _____

Income at Risk (i.e., deals that may not close on time): _____

Closed Deals This Month: _____

This Month in Review

What worked?

_____

_____

_____

_____

What didn't?

_____

_____

_____

_____

Keep:

_____
_____
_____
_____

Drop:

_____
_____
_____
_____

Three Micro-Goals for This Month:

1) _____
2) _____
3) _____

Market & Competitor Snapshot

New listings: _____

Closings: _____

Days on market: _____

Trend: _____

Competitor move worth noting: _____

Three "Get Out of the Office" Activities

Examples:
- Visit a local business owner to check in.
- Preview two new listings for market awareness.
- Walk your farm area and talk to three homeowners.
- Drop off a CMA packet to a warm lead.
- Attend one community or networking event.

1. _____

2. _____

3. _____

Month _____ Year_____

Form #1: Prospecting Worksheet

Your Hit List: Targets You Reached This Month

Activity	Week One	Week Two	Week Three	Week Four	Week Five	Total
Calls made						
Texts sent						
Emails sent						
Follow-ups completed						
Real conversations						
Appointments booked						

The 10 Connections that Mattered Most

       *Lead Type   Names(s) or Source   Notes

1) _____ _____ _____

2) _____ _____ _____

3) _____ _____ _____

4) _____ _____ _____

5) _____ _____ _____

6) _____ _____ _____

7) _____ _____ _____

8) _____ _____ _____

9) _____ _____ _____

10) _____ _____ _____

*Sphere of influence, online lead, open house, referral, past client, cold outreach, etc.

Your Pipeline Check

New leads added to CRM: _____

Warm leads contacted this month: _____

Cold leads reactivated: _____

Follow-up tasks scheduled for next month: _____

Quick Self-Assessment
(Circle one)

I stayed consistent:	YES	NO	SOMETIMES
I focused more on conversations than counting tasks:	YES	NO	SOMETIMES
I followed up when I said I would:	YES	NO	SOMETIMES
I protected my prospecting time:	YES	NO	SOMETIMES

What Moved the Needle this Month?

Which efforts generated the best conversations this month?

_____

_____

_____

_____

_____

Where did I lose focus or momentum and how can I gain it back?

_____

_____

_____

_____

_____

One adjustment I'll make next month:

_____

_____

_____

_____

_____

Form #2: Monthly Marketing Spend Tracker

Where Your Marketing Dollars are Going

Category	Amount Spent	Leads Generated	Notes
Ads – Facebook/Instagram	_____	_____	_____ _____
Ads – Google/YouTube	_____	_____	_____ _____
Print/Postcards	_____	_____	_____ _____
MLS/Tech Subscriptions	_____	_____	_____ _____
Lead Gen Platforms	_____	_____	_____ _____
Website/SEO	_____	_____	_____ _____
Email Marketing	_____	_____	_____ _____
Open House	_____	_____	_____ _____
Supplies	_____	_____	_____ _____
Client Gifts/Events	_____	_____	_____ _____
Misc.	_____	_____	_____ _____
TOTALS	_____	_____	_____ _____

Summary + Quick Calculations

Total Monthly Spend: $_____

Total Leads Generated: _____

Cost per Lead (CPL):
Total Spend ÷ Total Leads = $_____

Cost per Closing (CPC):
Total Spend ÷ # of Closings from This Month's Leads = $_____

Keep or Cut? ✂

Which expenses earned their keep this month?

_____
_____
_____
_____
_____

Which expenses didn't deliver and should be dropped next month?

_____
_____
_____
_____

What change will I make to improve ROI next month?

_____
_____
_____
_____
_____

Form #3: Financial Stability Check

Monthly Financial Snapshot

Opening Balance $ _____

Expected Income $ _____

Actual Income $ _____

Notes   _____

     _____

Fixed Expenses

Amount

Rent/Mortgage $ _____

Car Payment $ _____

Insurance $ _____

MLS/Association Dues $ _____

Phone/Internet $ _____

CRM/Software $ _____

Advertising Subscriptions $ _____

Utilities $ _____

Other $ _____

Discretionary Spending

Item	Amount
_____	$ _____
_____	$ _____
_____	$ _____
_____	$ _____
_____	$ _____
_____	$ _____

Debt/Savings Update

Debt Changes (increase or decrease)   _____

Current Savings Balance $ _____

Savings Added This Month $ _____

Red Flag Check

[ ] I spent more than I earned

[ ] I didn't track my expenses

[ ] I relied on credit to get through the month

[ ] My savings dropped instead of increasing

[ ] I struggled to cover fixed expenses

What's Working & What's Not

Where did I stay financially disciplined this month?

_____
_____
_____
_____
_____

Where did I lose focus or overspend?

_____
_____
_____
_____
_____

One adjustment I'll make next month:

_____
_____
_____
_____
_____

Form #4: Lead Conversion Log

Lead Name	Source	Date Recieved	First Contact Attempt	Follow-up Attempts	Appointment Set (Y/N)	Converted or Lost

Lead Details Snapshot

Lead Name	Source	Status

Your Follow-Up Check

New leads added this month: _____

Leads contacted within 24 hours: _____

Leads requiring additional follow-up: _____

Appointments scheduled: _____

Closed deals from this month's leads: _____

Quick Self-Assessment

I responded to leads quickly:	YES	NO	SOMETIMES
I stayed consistent with my follow-up:	YES	NO	SOMETIMES
I used the right number of touchpoints:	YES	NO	SOMETIMES
I handled objections clearly and confidently:	YES	NO	SOMETIMES
I protected my lead follow-up time:	YES	NO	SOMETIMES

What's Working & What's Not

What generated the best conversations this month?

_____

_____

_____

_____

_____

Where did my follow-up slow down or fall through?

_____

_____

_____

_____

_____

One small-but-mighty adjustment I will make next month:

_____

_____

_____

_____

_____

Form #5: Monthly Pipeline & Momentum Dashboard

Pipeline + Money Flow

Client	Source	Stage (New, Warm, Hot, Pending)	Actions Needed	Est. Close	Est. $	Confidence Level

Projected Income: _____

Income at Risk (i.e., deals that may not close on time): _____

Closed Deals This Month: _____

This Month in Review

What worked?

_____

_____

_____

_____

What didn't?

_____

_____

_____

_____

Keep:

_____

_____

_____

_____

Drop:

_____

_____

_____

_____

Three Micro-Goals for This Month:

1) _____

2) _____

3) _____

Market & Competitor Snapshot

New listings: _____

Closings: _____

Days on market: _____

Trend: _____

Competitor move worth noting: _____

Three "Get Out of the Office" Activities

Examples:
- Visit a local business owner to check in.
- Preview two new listings for market awareness.
- Walk your farm area and talk to three homeowners.
- Drop off a CMA packet to a warm lead.
- Attend one community or networking event.

1. _____

2. _____

3. _____

Month _____ Year_____

Form #1: Prospecting Worksheet

Your Hit List: Targets You Reached This Month

Activity	Week One	Week Two	Week Three	Week Four	Week Five	Total
Calls made						
Texts sent						
Emails sent						
Follow-ups completed						
Real conversations						
Appointments booked						

The 10 Connections that Mattered Most

	*Lead Type	Names(s) or Source	Notes
1)			
2)			
3)			
4)			
5)			
6)			
7)			
8)			
9)			
10)			

*Sphere of influence, online lead, open house, referral, past client, cold outreach, etc.

Your Pipeline Check

New leads added to CRM: _____

Warm leads contacted this month: _____

Cold leads reactivated: _____

Follow-up tasks scheduled for next month: _____

Quick Self-Assessment
(Circle one)

I stayed consistent:	YES	NO	SOMETIMES
I focused more on conversations than counting tasks:	YES	NO	SOMETIMES
I followed up when I said I would:	YES	NO	SOMETIMES
I protected my prospecting time:	YES	NO	SOMETIMES

What Moved the Needle this Month?

Which efforts generated the best conversations this month?

_____
_____
_____
_____
_____

Where did I lose focus or momentum and how can I gain it back?

_____
_____
_____
_____
_____

One adjustment I'll make next month:

_____
_____
_____
_____
_____

Form #2: Monthly Marketing Spend Tracker

Where Your Marketing Dollars are Going

Category	Amount Spent	Leads Generated	Notes
Ads – Facebook/Instagram			
Ads – Google/YouTube			
Print/Postcards			
MLS/Tech Subscriptions			
Lead Gen Platforms			
Website/SEO			
Email Marketing			
Open House			
Supplies			
Client Gifts/Events			
Misc.			
TOTALS			

Summary + Quick Calculations

Total Monthly Spend: $_____

Total Leads Generated: _____

Cost per Lead (CPL):
Total Spend ÷ Total Leads = $_____

Cost per Closing (CPC):
Total Spend ÷ # of Closings from This Month's Leads = $_____

Keep or Cut?

Which expenses earned their keep this month?

_____
_____
_____
_____
_____

Which expenses didn't deliver and should be dropped next month?

_____
_____
_____
_____
_____

What change will I make to improve ROI next month?

_____
_____
_____
_____
_____

Form #3: Financial Stability Check

Monthly Financial Snapshot

Opening Balance $ _____

Expected Income $ _____

Actual Income $ _____

Notes _____

_____

Fixed Expenses

	Amount
Rent/Mortgage	$ _____
Car Payment	$ _____
Insurance	$ _____
MLS/Association Dues	$ _____
Phone/Internet	$ _____
CRM/Software	$ _____
Advertising Subscriptions	$ _____
Utilities	$ _____
Other	$ _____

Discretionary Spending

Item	Amount
_____	$ _____
_____	$ _____
_____	$ _____
_____	$ _____
_____	$ _____
_____	$ _____

Debt/Savings Update

Debt Changes (increase or decrease)   _____

Current Savings Balance $ _____

Savings Added This Month $ _____

Red Flag Check

[ ] I spent more than I earned

[ ] I didn't track my expenses

[ ] I relied on credit to get through the month

[ ] My savings dropped instead of increasing

[ ] I struggled to cover fixed expenses

What's Working & What's Not

Where did I stay financially disciplined this month?

_____
_____
_____
_____
_____

Where did I lose focus or overspend?

_____
_____
_____
_____
_____

One adjustment I'll make next month:

_____
_____
_____
_____
_____

Form #4: Lead Conversion Log

Lead Name	Source	Date Recieved	First Contact Attempt	Follow-up Attempts	Appointment Set (Y/N)	Converted or Lost

Lead Details Snapshot

Lead Name	Source	Status

Your Follow-Up Check

New leads added this month: _____

Leads contacted within 24 hours: _____

Leads requiring additional follow-up: _____

Appointments scheduled: _____

Closed deals from this month's leads: _____

Quick Self-Assessment

I responded to leads quickly:	YES	NO	SOMETIMES
I stayed consistent with my follow-up:	YES	NO	SOMETIMES
I used the right number of touchpoints:	YES	NO	SOMETIMES
I handled objections clearly and confidently:	YES	NO	SOMETIMES
I protected my lead follow-up time:	YES	NO	SOMETIMES

What's Working & What's Not

What generated the best conversations this month?

_____

_____

_____

_____

_____

Where did my follow-up slow down or fall through?

_____

_____

_____

_____

_____

One small-but-mighty adjustment I will make next month:

_____

_____

_____

_____

_____

Form #5: Monthly Pipeline & Momentum Dashboard

Pipeline + Money Flow

Client	Source	Stage (New, Warm, Hot, Pending)	Actions Needed	Est. Close	Est. $	Confidence Level

Projected Income: _____

Income at Risk (i.e., deals that may not close on time): _____

Closed Deals This Month: _____

This Month in Review

What worked?

_____
_____
_____
_____

What didn't?

_____
_____
_____
_____

Keep:

_____
_____
_____
_____

Drop:

_____
_____
_____
_____

Three Micro-Goals for This Month:

1) _____
2) _____
3) _____

Market & Competitor Snapshot

New listings: _____

Closings: _____

Days on market: _____

Trend: _____

Competitor move worth noting: _____

Three "Get Out of the Office" Activities

Examples:
- Visit a local business owner to check in.
- Preview two new listings for market awareness.
- Walk your farm area and talk to three homeowners.
- Drop off a CMA packet to a warm lead.
- Attend one community or networking event.

1. _____

2. _____

3. _____

Month _____ Year_____

Form #1: Prospecting Worksheet

Your Hit List: Targets You Reached This Month

Activity	Week One	Week Two	Week Three	Week Four	Week Five	Total
Calls made						
Texts sent						
Emails sent						
Follow-ups completed						
Real conversations						
Appointments booked						

The 10 Connections that Mattered Most

         *Lead Type   Names(s) or Source   Notes

1) _____ _____ _____

2) _____ _____ _____

3) _____ _____ _____

4) _____ _____ _____

5) _____ _____ _____

6) _____ _____ _____

7) _____ _____ _____

8) _____ _____ _____

9) _____ _____ _____

10) _____ _____ _____

*Sphere of influence, online lead, open house, referral, past client, cold outreach, etc.

Your Pipeline Check

New leads added to CRM: _____

Warm leads contacted this month: _____

Cold leads reactivated: _____

Follow-up tasks scheduled for next month: _____

Quick Self-Assessment
(Circle one)

I stayed consistent:	YES	NO	SOMETIMES
I focused more on conversations than counting tasks:	YES	NO	SOMETIMES
I followed up when I said I would:	YES	NO	SOMETIMES
I protected my prospecting time:	YES	NO	SOMETIMES

What Moved the Needle this Month?

Which efforts generated the best conversations this month?

_____
_____
_____
_____
_____

Where did I lose focus or momentum and how can I gain it back?

_____
_____
_____
_____
_____

One adjustment I'll make next month:

_____
_____
_____
_____
_____

Form #2: Monthly Marketing Spend Tracker

Where Your Marketing Dollars are Going

Category	Amount Spent	Leads Generated	Notes
Ads – Facebook/Instagram	_____	_____	_____ _____
Ads – Google/YouTube	_____	_____	_____ _____
Print/Postcards	_____	_____	_____ _____
MLS/Tech Subscriptions	_____	_____	_____ _____
Lead Gen Platforms	_____	_____	_____ _____
Website/SEO	_____	_____	_____ _____
Email Marketing	_____	_____	_____ _____
Open House	_____	_____	_____ _____
Supplies	_____	_____	_____ _____
Client Gifts/Events	_____	_____	_____ _____
Misc.	_____	_____	_____ _____
TOTALS	_____	_____	_____ _____

Summary + Quick Calculations

Total Monthly Spend: $_____

Total Leads Generated: _____

Cost per Lead (CPL):
Total Spend ÷ Total Leads = $_____

Cost per Closing (CPC):
Total Spend ÷ # of Closings from This Month's Leads = $_____

Keep or Cut?

Which expenses earned their keep this month?

_____
_____
_____
_____
_____

Which expenses didn't deliver and should be dropped next month?

_____
_____
_____
_____
_____

What change will I make to improve ROI next month?

_____
_____
_____
_____
_____

Form #3: Financial Stability Check

Monthly Financial Snapshot

Opening Balance $ _____

Expected Income $ _____

Actual Income $ _____

Notes _____

_____

Fixed Expenses

Amount

Rent/Mortgage $ _____

Car Payment $ _____

Insurance $ _____

MLS/Association Dues $ _____

Phone/Internet $ _____

CRM/Software $ _____

Advertising Subscriptions $ _____

Utilities $ _____

Other $ _____

Discretionary Spending

Item **Amount**

_____ $ _____

_____ $ _____

_____ $ _____

_____ $ _____

_____ $ _____

_____ $ _____

Debt/Savings Update

Debt Changes (increase or decrease)   _____

Current Savings Balance $ _____

Savings Added This Month $ _____

Red Flag Check

[ ] I spent more than I earned

[ ] I didn't track my expenses

[ ] I relied on credit to get through the month

[ ] My savings dropped instead of increasing

[ ] I struggled to cover fixed expenses

What's Working & What's Not

Where did I stay financially disciplined this month?

_____
_____
_____
_____
_____

Where did I lose focus or overspend?

_____
_____
_____
_____
_____

One adjustment I'll make next month:

_____
_____
_____
_____
_____

Form #4: Lead Conversion Log

Lead Name	Source	Date Recieved	First Contact Attempt	Follow-up Attempts	Appointment Set (Y/N)	Converted or Lost

Lead Details Snapshot

Lead Name	Source	Status

Your Follow-Up Check

New leads added this month: _____

Leads contacted within 24 hours: _____

Leads requiring additional follow-up: _____

Appointments scheduled: _____

Closed deals from this month's leads: _____

Quick Self-Assessment

I responded to leads quickly: YES   NO   SOMETIMES

I stayed consistent with my follow-up: YES   NO   SOMETIMES

I used the right number of touchpoints: YES   NO   SOMETIMES

I handled objections clearly and confidently: YES   NO   SOMETIMES

I protected my lead follow-up time: YES   NO   SOMETIMES

What's Working & What's Not

What generated the best conversations this month?

_____

_____

_____

_____

_____

Where did my follow-up slow down or fall through?

_____

_____

_____

_____

_____

One small-but-mighty adjustment I will make next month:

_____

_____

_____

_____

_____

Form #5: Monthly Pipeline & Momentum Dashboard

Pipeline + Money Flow

Client	Source	Stage (New, Warm, Hot, Pending)	Actions Needed	Est. Close	Est. $	Confidence Level

Projected Income: _____

Income at Risk (i.e., deals that may not close on time): _____

Closed Deals This Month: _____

This Month in Review

What worked?

_____

_____

_____

_____

What didn't?

_____

_____

_____

_____

Keep:

_____
_____
_____
_____

Drop:

_____
_____
_____
_____

Three Micro-Goals for This Month:

1) _____
2) _____
3) _____

Market & Competitor Snapshot

New listings: _____

Closings: _____

Days on market: _____

Trend: _____

Competitor move worth noting: _____

Three "Get Out of the Office" Activities

Examples:
- Visit a local business owner to check in.
- Preview two new listings for market awareness.
- Walk your farm area and talk to three homeowners.
- Drop off a CMA packet to a warm lead.
- Attend one community or networking event.

1. _____

2. _____

3. _____

Month _____ Year_____

Form #1: Prospecting Worksheet

Your Hit List: Targets You Reached This Month

Activity	Week One	Week Two	Week Three	Week Four	Week Five	Total
Calls made						
Texts sent						
Emails sent						
Follow-ups completed						
Real conversations						
Appointments booked						

The 10 Connections that Mattered Most

	*Lead Type	Names(s) or Source	Notes
1)	_____	_____	_____
2)	_____	_____	_____
3)	_____	_____	_____
4)	_____	_____	_____
5)	_____	_____	_____
6)	_____	_____	_____
7)	_____	_____	_____
8)	_____	_____	_____
9)	_____	_____	_____
10)	_____	_____	_____

*Sphere of influence, online lead, open house, referral, past client, cold outreach, etc.

Your Pipeline Check

New leads added to CRM: _____

Warm leads contacted this month: _____

Cold leads reactivated: _____

Follow-up tasks scheduled for next month: _____

Quick Self-Assessment
(Circle one)

I stayed consistent:	YES	NO	SOMETIMES
I focused more on conversations than counting tasks:	YES	NO	SOMETIMES
I followed up when I said I would:	YES	NO	SOMETIMES
I protected my prospecting time:	YES	NO	SOMETIMES

What Moved the Needle this Month?

Which efforts generated the best conversations this month?

_____
_____
_____
_____
_____

Where did I lose focus or momentum and how can I gain it back?

_____
_____
_____
_____
_____

One adjustment I'll make next month:

_____
_____
_____
_____
_____

Form #2: Monthly Marketing Spend Tracker

Where Your Marketing Dollars are Going

Category	Amount Spent	Leads Generated	Notes
Ads - Facebook/Instagram	_____	_____	_____
			_____
Ads - Google/YouTube	_____	_____	_____
			_____
Print/Postcards	_____	_____	_____
			_____
MLS/Tech Subscriptions	_____	_____	_____
			_____
Lead Gen Platforms	_____	_____	_____
			_____
Website/SEO	_____	_____	_____
			_____
Email Marketing	_____	_____	_____
			_____
Open House	_____	_____	_____
			_____
Supplies	_____	_____	_____
			_____
Client Gifts/Events	_____	_____	_____
			_____
Misc.	_____	_____	_____
			_____
TOTALS	_____	_____	_____
			_____

Summary + Quick Calculations

Total Monthly Spend: $_____

Total Leads Generated: _____

Cost per Lead (CPL):
Total Spend ÷ Total Leads = $_____

Cost per Closing (CPC):
Total Spend ÷ # of Closings from This Month's Leads = $_____

Keep or Cut? ✂

Which expenses earned their keep this month?

_____
_____
_____
_____
_____

Which expenses didn't deliver and should be dropped next month?

_____
_____
_____
_____
_____

What change will I make to improve ROI next month?

_____
_____
_____
_____
_____

Form #3: Financial Stability Check

Monthly Financial Snapshot

Opening Balance $ _____

Expected Income $ _____

Actual Income $ _____

Notes   _____

_____

Fixed Expenses

Amount

Rent/Mortgage $ _____

Car Payment $ _____

Insurance $ _____

MLS/Association Dues $ _____

Phone/Internet $ _____

CRM/Software $ _____

Advertising Subscriptions $ _____

Utilities $ _____

Other $ _____

Discretionary Spending

Item   **Amount**

_____ $ _____

_____ $ _____

_____ $ _____

_____ $ _____

_____ $ _____

_____ $ _____

Debt/Savings Update

Debt Changes (increase or decrease) _____

Current Savings Balance $ _____

Savings Added This Month $ _____

Red Flag Check

[ ] I spent more than I earned

[ ] I didn't track my expenses

[ ] I relied on credit to get through the month

[ ] My savings dropped instead of increasing

[ ] I struggled to cover fixed expenses

What's Working & What's Not

Where did I stay financially disciplined this month?

_____
_____
_____
_____
_____

Where did I lose focus or overspend?

_____
_____
_____
_____
_____

One adjustment I'll make next month:

_____
_____
_____
_____
_____

Form #4: Lead Conversion Log

Lead Name	Source	Date Recieved	First Contact Attempt	Follow-up Attempts	Appointment Set (Y/N)	Converted or Lost

Lead Details Snapshot

Lead Name	Source	Status

Your Follow-Up Check

New leads added this month: _____

Leads contacted within 24 hours: _____

Leads requiring additional follow-up: _____

Appointments scheduled: _____

Closed deals from this month's leads: _____

Quick Self-Assessment

I responded to leads quickly:	YES	NO	SOMETIMES
I stayed consistent with my follow-up:	YES	NO	SOMETIMES
I used the right number of touchpoints:	YES	NO	SOMETIMES
I handled objections clearly and confidently:	YES	NO	SOMETIMES
I protected my lead follow-up time:	YES	NO	SOMETIMES

What's Working & What's Not

What generated the best conversations this month?

_____

_____

_____

_____

_____

Where did my follow-up slow down or fall through?

_____

_____

_____

_____

_____

One small-but-mighty adjustment I will make next month:

_____

_____

_____

_____

_____

Form #5: Monthly Pipeline & Momentum Dashboard

Pipeline + Money Flow

Client	Source	Stage (New, Warm, Hot, Pending)	Actions Needed	Est. Close	Est. $	Confidence Level

Projected Income: _____

Income at Risk (i.e., deals that may not close on time): _____

Closed Deals This Month: _____

This Month in Review

What worked?

_____

_____

_____

_____

What didn't?

_____

_____

_____

_____

Keep:

_____

_____

_____

_____

Drop:

_____

_____

_____

_____

Three Micro-Goals for This Month:

1) _____

2) _____

3) _____

Market & Competitor Snapshot

New listings: _____

Closings: _____

Days on market: _____

Trend: _____

Competitor move worth noting: _____

Three "Get Out of the Office" Activities

Examples:
- Visit a local business owner to check in.
- Preview two new listings for market awareness.
- Walk your farm area and talk to three homeowners.
- Drop off a CMA packet to a warm lead.
- Attend one community or networking event.

1. _____

2. _____

3. _____

Month _____ Year_____

Form #1: Prospecting Worksheet

Your Hit List: Targets You Reached This Month

Activity	Week One	Week Two	Week Three	Week Four	Week Five	Total
Calls made						
Texts sent						
Emails sent						
Follow-ups completed						
Real conversations						
Appointments booked						

The 10 Connections that Mattered Most

	*Lead Type	Names(s) or Source	Notes
1)	_____	_____	_____
2)	_____	_____	_____
3)	_____	_____	_____
4)	_____	_____	_____
5)	_____	_____	_____
6)	_____	_____	_____
7)	_____	_____	_____
8)	_____	_____	_____
9)	_____	_____	_____
10)	_____	_____	_____

*Sphere of influence, online lead, open house, referral, past client, cold outreach, etc.

Your Pipeline Check

New leads added to CRM: _____

Warm leads contacted this month: _____

Cold leads reactivated: _____

Follow-up tasks scheduled for next month: _____

Quick Self-Assessment
(Circle one)

I stayed consistent:	YES	NO	SOMETIMES
I focused more on conversations than counting tasks:	YES	NO	SOMETIMES
I followed up when I said I would:	YES	NO	SOMETIMES
I protected my prospecting time:	YES	NO	SOMETIMES

What Moved the Needle this Month?

Which efforts generated the best conversations this month?

_____

_____

_____

_____

_____

Where did I lose focus or momentum and how can I gain it back?

_____

_____

_____

_____

_____

One adjustment I'll make next month:

_____

_____

_____

_____

_____

Form #2: Monthly Marketing Spend Tracker

Where Your Marketing Dollars are Going

Category	Amount Spent	Leads Generated	Notes
Ads – Facebook/Instagram	_____	_____	_____
			_____
Ads – Google/YouTube	_____	_____	_____
			_____
Print/Postcards	_____	_____	_____
			_____
MLS/Tech Subscriptions	_____	_____	_____
			_____
Lead Gen Platforms	_____	_____	_____
			_____
Website/SEO	_____	_____	_____
			_____
Email Marketing	_____	_____	_____
			_____
Open House	_____	_____	_____
			_____
Supplies	_____	_____	_____
			_____
Client Gifts/Events	_____	_____	_____
			_____
Misc.	_____	_____	_____
			_____
TOTALS	_____	_____	_____
			_____

Summary + Quick Calculations

Total Monthly Spend: $_____

Total Leads Generated: _____

Cost per Lead (CPL):
Total Spend ÷ Total Leads = $_____

Cost per Closing (CPC):
Total Spend ÷ # of Closings from This Month's Leads = $_____

Keep or Cut?

Which expenses earned their keep this month?

_____

_____

_____

_____

_____

Which expenses didn't deliver and should be dropped next month?

_____

_____

_____

_____

_____

What change will I make to improve ROI next month?

_____

_____

_____

_____

_____

Form #3: Financial Stability Check

Monthly Financial Snapshot

Opening Balance $ _____

Expected Income $ _____

Actual Income $ _____

Notes   _____

_____

Fixed Expenses

Amount

Rent/Mortgage $ _____

Car Payment $ _____

Insurance $ _____

MLS/Association Dues $ _____

Phone/Internet $ _____

CRM/Software $ _____

Advertising Subscriptions $ _____

Utilities $ _____

Other $ _____

Discretionary Spending

Item   **Amount**

_____ $ _____

_____ $ _____

_____ $ _____

_____ $ _____

_____ $ _____

_____ $ _____

Debt/Savings Update

Debt Changes (increase or decrease) _____

Current Savings Balance $ _____

Savings Added This Month $ _____

Red Flag Check

[ ] I spent more than I earned

[ ] I didn't track my expenses

[ ] I relied on credit to get through the month

[ ] My savings dropped instead of increasing

[ ] I struggled to cover fixed expenses

What's Working & What's Not

Where did I stay financially disciplined this month?

_____
_____
_____
_____
_____

Where did I lose focus or overspend?

_____
_____
_____
_____
_____

One adjustment I'll make next month:

_____
_____
_____
_____
_____

Form #4: Lead Conversion Log

Lead Name	Source	Date Recieved	First Contact Attempt	Follow-up Attempts	Appointment Set (Y/N)	Converted or Lost

Lead Details Snapshot

Lead Name	Source	Status

Your Follow-Up Check

New leads added this month: _____

Leads contacted within 24 hours: _____

Leads requiring additional follow-up: _____

Appointments scheduled: _____

Closed deals from this month's leads: _____

Quick Self-Assessment

I responded to leads quickly:	YES	NO	SOMETIMES
I stayed consistent with my follow-up:	YES	NO	SOMETIMES
I used the right number of touchpoints:	YES	NO	SOMETIMES
I handled objections clearly and confidently:	YES	NO	SOMETIMES
I protected my lead follow-up time:	YES	NO	SOMETIMES

What's Working & What's Not

What generated the best conversations this month?

_____

_____

_____

_____

_____

Where did my follow-up slow down or fall through?

_____

_____

_____

_____

_____

One small-but-mighty adjustment I will make next month:

_____

_____

_____

_____

_____

Form #5: Monthly Pipeline & Momentum Dashboard

Pipeline + Money Flow

Client	Source	Stage (New, Warm, Hot, Pending)	Actions Needed	Est. Close	Est. $	Confidence Level

Projected Income: _____

Income at Risk (i.e., deals that may not close on time): _____

Closed Deals This Month: _____

This Month in Review

What worked?

_____

_____

_____

_____

What didn't?

_____

_____

_____

_____

Keep:

_____
_____
_____
_____

Drop:

_____
_____
_____
_____

Three Micro-Goals for This Month:

1) _____

2) _____

3) _____

Market & Competitor Snapshot

New listings: _____

Closings: _____

Days on market: _____

Trend: _____

Competitor move worth noting: _____

Three "Get Out of the Office" Activities

Examples:
- Visit a local business owner to check in.
- Preview two new listings for market awareness.
- Walk your farm area and talk to three homeowners.
- Drop off a CMA packet to a warm lead.
- Attend one community or networking event.

1. _____

2. _____

3. _____

Month _____ Year_____

Form #1: Prospecting Worksheet

Your Hit List: Targets You Reached This Month

Activity	Week One	Week Two	Week Three	Week Four	Week Five	Total
Calls made						
Texts sent						
Emails sent						
Follow-ups completed						
Real conversations						
Appointments booked						

The 10 Connections that Mattered Most

	*Lead Type	Names(s) or Source	Notes
1)	_____	_____	_____
2)	_____	_____	_____
3)	_____	_____	_____
4)	_____	_____	_____
5)	_____	_____	_____
6)	_____	_____	_____
7)	_____	_____	_____
8)	_____	_____	_____
9)	_____	_____	_____
10)	_____	_____	_____

*Sphere of influence, online lead, open house, referral, past client, cold outreach, etc.

Your Pipeline Check

New leads added to CRM: _____

Warm leads contacted this month: _____

Cold leads reactivated: _____

Follow-up tasks scheduled for next month: _____

Quick Self-Assessment
(Circle one)

I stayed consistent:	YES	NO	SOMETIMES
I focused more on conversations than counting tasks:	YES	NO	SOMETIMES
I followed up when I said I would:	YES	NO	SOMETIMES
I protected my prospecting time:	YES	NO	SOMETIMES

What Moved the Needle this Month?

Which efforts generated the best conversations this month?

_____
_____
_____
_____
_____

Where did I lose focus or momentum and how can I gain it back?

_____
_____
_____
_____
_____

One adjustment I'll make next month:

_____
_____
_____
_____
_____

Form #2: Monthly Marketing Spend Tracker

Where Your Marketing Dollars are Going

Category	Amount Spent	Leads Generated	Notes
Ads - Facebook/Instagram	_____	_____	_____ _____
Ads - Google/YouTube	_____	_____	_____ _____
Print/Postcards	_____	_____	_____ _____
MLS/Tech Subscriptions	_____	_____	_____ _____
Lead Gen Platforms	_____	_____	_____ _____
Website/SEO	_____	_____	_____ _____
Email Marketing	_____	_____	_____ _____
Open House	_____	_____	_____ _____
Supplies	_____	_____	_____ _____
Client Gifts/Events	_____	_____	_____ _____
Misc.	_____	_____	_____ _____
TOTALS	_____	_____	_____ _____

Summary + Quick Calculations

Total Monthly Spend: $_____

Total Leads Generated: _____

Cost per Lead (CPL):
Total Spend ÷ Total Leads = $_____

Cost per Closing (CPC):
Total Spend ÷ # of Closings from This Month's Leads = $_____

Keep or Cut? ✂

Which expenses earned their keep this month?

_____
_____
_____
_____
_____

Which expenses didn't deliver and should be dropped next month?

_____
_____
_____
_____
_____

What change will I make to improve ROI next month?

_____
_____
_____
_____
_____

Form #3: Financial Stability Check

Monthly Financial Snapshot

Opening Balance $ \underline{\hspace{6cm}}

Expected Income $ \underline{\hspace{6cm}}

Actual Income $ \underline{\hspace{6cm}}

Notes   \underline{\hspace{6cm}}

\underline{\hspace{6cm}}

Fixed Expenses

Amount

Rent/Mortgage $ \underline{\hspace{6cm}}

Car Payment $ \underline{\hspace{6cm}}

Insurance $ \underline{\hspace{6cm}}

MLS/Association Dues $ \underline{\hspace{6cm}}

Phone/Internet $ \underline{\hspace{6cm}}

CRM/Software $ \underline{\hspace{6cm}}

Advertising Subscriptions $ \underline{\hspace{6cm}}

Utilities $ \underline{\hspace{6cm}}

Other $ \underline{\hspace{6cm}}

Discretionary Spending

Item   **Amount**

\underline{\hspace{5cm}} $ \underline{\hspace{6cm}}

\underline{\hspace{5cm}} $ \underline{\hspace{6cm}}

\underline{\hspace{5cm}} $ \underline{\hspace{6cm}}

\underline{\hspace{5cm}} $ \underline{\hspace{6cm}}

\underline{\hspace{5cm}} $ \underline{\hspace{6cm}}

\underline{\hspace{5cm}} $ \underline{\hspace{6cm}}

Debt/Savings Update

Debt Changes (increase or decrease)   _____

Current Savings Balance $ _____

Savings Added This Month $ _____

Red Flag Check

[ ] I spent more than I earned

[ ] I didn't track my expenses

[ ] I relied on credit to get through the month

[ ] My savings dropped instead of increasing

[ ] I struggled to cover fixed expenses

What's Working & What's Not

Where did I stay financially disciplined this month?

_____
_____
_____
_____
_____

Where did I lose focus or overspend?

_____
_____
_____
_____
_____

One adjustment I'll make next month:

_____
_____
_____
_____
_____

Form #4: Lead Conversion Log

Lead Name	Source	Date Recieved	First Contact Attempt	Follow-up Attempts	Appointment Set (Y/N)	Converted or Lost

Lead Details Snapshot

Lead Name	Source	Status

Your Follow-Up Check

New leads added this month: _____

Leads contacted within 24 hours: _____

Leads requiring additional follow-up: _____

Appointments scheduled: _____

Closed deals from this month's leads: _____

Quick Self-Assessment

I responded to leads quickly: YES   NO   SOMETIMES

I stayed consistent with my follow-up: YES   NO   SOMETIMES

I used the right number of touchpoints: YES   NO   SOMETIMES

I handled objections clearly and confidently: YES   NO   SOMETIMES

I protected my lead follow-up time: YES   NO   SOMETIMES

What's Working & What's Not

What generated the best conversations this month?

_____

_____

_____

_____

_____

Where did my follow-up slow down or fall through?

_____

_____

_____

_____

_____

One small-but-mighty adjustment I will make next month:

_____

_____

_____

_____

_____

Form #5: Monthly Pipeline & Momentum Dashboard

Pipeline + Money Flow

Client	Source	Stage (New, Warm, Hot, Pending)	Actions Needed	Est. Close	Est. $	Confidence Level

Projected Income: _____

Income at Risk (i.e., deals that may not close on time): _____

Closed Deals This Month: _____

This Month in Review

What worked?

_____

_____

_____

_____

What didn't?

_____

_____

_____

_____

Keep:

_____
_____
_____
_____

Drop:

_____
_____
_____
_____

Three Micro-Goals for This Month:

1) _____
2) _____
3) _____

Market & Competitor Snapshot

New listings: _____

Closings: _____

Days on market: _____

Trend: _____

Competitor move worth noting: _____

Three "Get Out of the Office" Activities

Examples:
- Visit a local business owner to check in.
- Preview two new listings for market awareness.
- Walk your farm area and talk to three homeowners.
- Drop off a CMA packet to a warm lead.
- Attend one community or networking event.

1. _____

2. _____

3. _____

Turn Consistency into Competitive Advantage

When you got your real estate license, you moved into a field that rewards professionals who show up, stay organized and keep moving when the day pulls them in every direction. The forms in this workbook give you a steady view of your business so you can stay focused on building relationships and keeping your client pipeline filled.

When you use the forms month after month, you'll feel more confident in every move you make in your business. For example:

- You'll notice patterns sooner and adjust before small issues escalate.
- You'll know which conversations matter most and which ones you can safely ignore.
- You'll handle slow stretches with more control because you'll see where your stand (instead of relying on guesswork).

Growth comes from building simple habits that you repeat over time. If you want deeper structure to support this system, the 20th Anniversary Edition of *The Real Estate Agent's Business Planner* pairs well with this workbook. The planner helps you set your direction and this workbook helps you follow through one month at a time.

Use them together and you'll win more clients, close more deals and make moves that produce real results.

Good luck!

Want the Full Framework Behind This Workbook?

If this workbook helped you stay organized and take consistent action, the 20th Anniversary Edition of *The Real Estate Agent's Business Planner* shows how those actions connect to a complete real estate business.

It covers the systems behind lead generation, client management and long-term income growth. You get:

- A clear path from getting licensed to closing your first deal
- Straight talk on how the business side of real estate actually works
- Practical guidance on generating leads and managing clients
- Proven strategies for organizing your time, priorities and pipeline
- Access to free digital planning tools that support the system

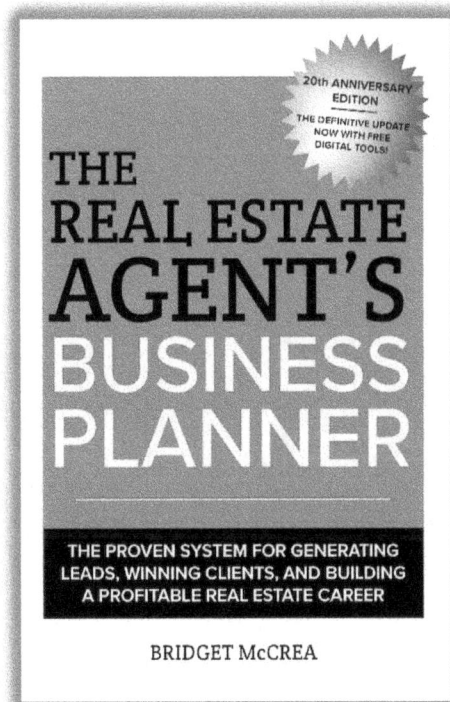

Ready to see the system in full?
Check out *The Real Estate Agent's Business Planner* on Amazon.

Bulk orders: For brokerages, teams and training programs, bulk paperback orders are available through Ingram. **ISBN: 978-0997045499**

About the Author

First of all, much gratitude for allowing me to play a small role in your new or growing real estate career. Know that I <u>do not</u> take that trust and responsibility lightly.

I'm Bridget McCrea. I've hustled through dead-end jobs, stretched a bank account that was almost empty, raised a toddler while chasing deadlines and built a business with nothing but determination, a desktop and a Texas Instruments 1200-baud modem at my kitchen table. For more than three decades I've been telling the real stories of entrepreneurs who took the same unpredictable path.

That work led to opportunities I never expected. I wrote *The Real Estate Agent's Business Plan* (and later acquired the rights to update it myself under the StrongTide Press imprint), followed by *The Real Estate Agent's Field Guide, The Home Buyer's Question and Answer Book* and *The RE/MAX Home Buyer's Survival Guide.* Wiley & Co. also contracted me to write *Second Homes for Dummies* and I've written for REALTOR magazine, Florida REALTOR and Texas REALTOR. I've been a REALTOR and a real estate office manager and along the way gained a ground-level view of what works in this business.

Three things I love most about being an entrepreneur & writer:

1. **Building something out of scraps.** I started with little more than grit, a toddler on my hip and a nearly empty bank account. I turned it into a business that lasted.

2. **Getting a front-row seat to other people's journeys**. From sitting across the table from inspiring female leaders like Mindy Grossman to hearing how R.W. Garcia's founders came up with the idea for tortilla salad strips, I've seen firsthand what it really takes to create something that lasts.

3. **Turning lessons into tools that help others**. Whether it's writing seven books, crafting a Dummies guide for Wiley or developing content for well-known companies like Toyota, Panasonic and SAP, I love distilling hard-won insights into something others can actually use.

I've written for some big-name media outlets, picked up a few awards along the way and published books that people still keep on their shelves. But the real win is seeing readers like you put the lessons to work. If *The Real Estate Agent's 12-Month Planning Workbook* helps you take even one solid step toward building your own successful real estate career, then it's done its job.

More from the StrongTide Press Library

The Real Estate Agent's Business Planner:
The Proven System for Generating Leads, Winning Clients and Building
a Profitable Real Estate Career

Your First Business Blueprint:
How to Plan, Launch and Grow a Profitable Small Business

Swift Success Guides
Blueprints Beat Cocktail Napkins:
How to Create a Winning Business Plan for Growth and Profit

★ **Coming Soon** ★
The Small Business Growth Blueprint:
How to Grow Your Business by Turning Customers Into Lifelong Fans

Share Your Experience & Help Others Start Smart

Starting a new real estate career isn't easy. I know firsthand how overwhelming it can feel. If *The Real Estate Agent's 12-Month Planning Workbook* helped you plan, launch or grow your real estate career, would you take a minute to share that in an Amazon review?

Your words can encourage the next real estate agent who's wondering whether they have what it takes. Reviews help others discover the book, see what's possible and take their first step.

Every review adds to a growing community of new real estate agents who are learning, building and succeeding together. I'd love for you to be part of it.